anything

D0554857

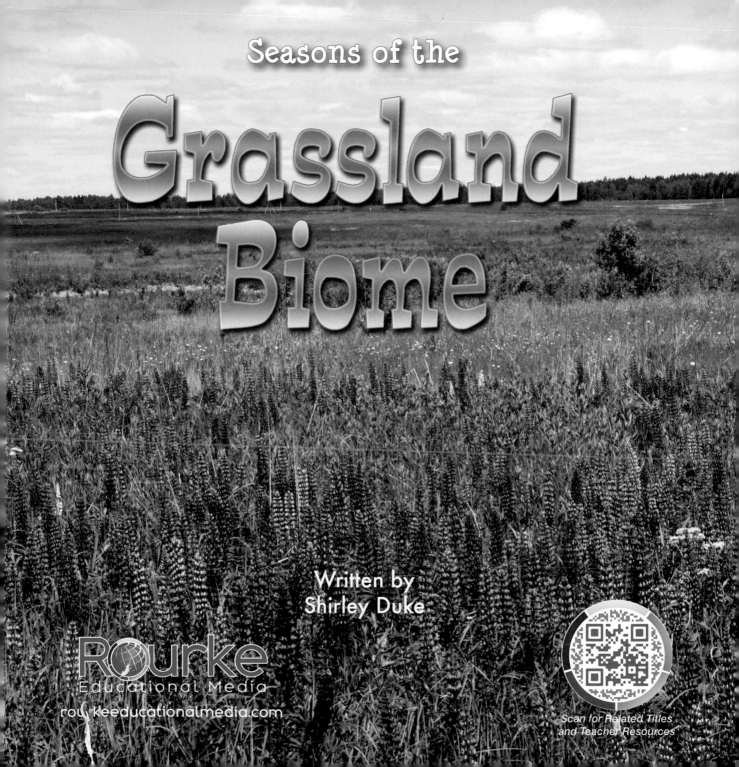

Seasons of the Grassland Biome

Written by
Shirley Duke

Rourke
Educational Media

rourkeeducationalmedia.com

www.rourkeeducationalmedia.com

PHOTO CREDITS: Cover: Nico Smit; Title Page © svic; Page 4 © Lockenes, map © Christian Lopetz, notebook © PixelEmbargo; Page 5 © spirit of america; Page 6 © James Mattil; Page 7 © Krzysztof Wiktor; Page 8 © 2009fotofriends; Page 9 © peresanz; Page 9 inset photo © Larry Lamsa; Page 10 © joloei, inset photos Chhe; Page 11 © Pefkos; Page 12 © 2009fotofriends; Page 12/13 © John Wollwerth; Page 14 © gallofoto; Page 14 inset photo © Anatoliy Lukich; Page 15 © Tom Reichner; Page 16 © balounm; Page 17 © Tony Campbell; Page 18 © GoodMood Photo; Page 19 © Cody Wheeler; Page 20 © Zack Frank; Page 21 © Goodluz;

Edited by Jill Sherman

Cover design by Renee Brady
Interior design by Nicola Stratford bdpublishing.com

Library of Congress PCN Data

Seasons of the Grassland Biome / Shirley Duke
(Biomes)
ISBN 978-1-62169-900-2 (hard cover)
ISBN 978-1-62169-795-4 (soft cover)
ISBN 978-1-62717-007-9 (e-Book)
Library of Congress Control Number: 2013936816

Also Available as:
ROURKE'S
e-Books

Rourke Educational Media
Printed in the United States of America,
North Mankato, Minnesota

Rourke
Educational Media

rourkeeducationalmedia.com

customerservice@rourkeeducationalmedia.com • PO Box 643328 Vero Beach, Florida 32964

Table of Contents

Grassy and Wide

What covers wide open **grasslands**?

You guessed it, grasses!

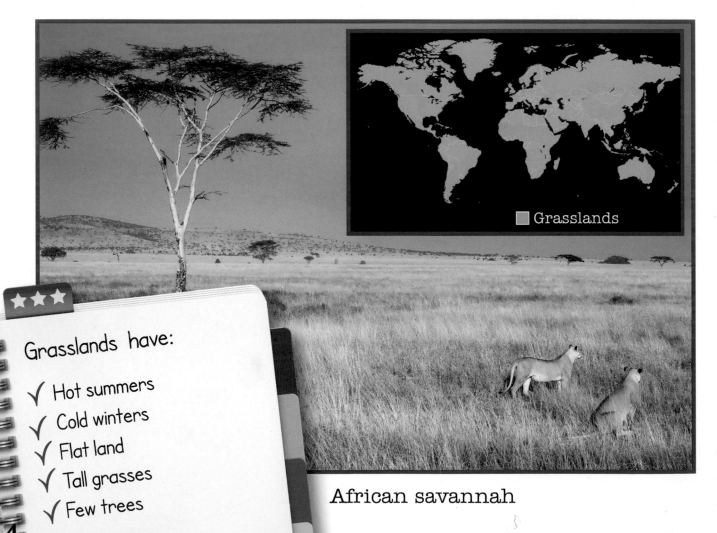

Grasslands

Grasslands have:

✓ Hot summers
✓ Cold winters
✓ Flat land
✓ Tall grasses
✓ Few trees

African savannah

Grasslands have cold winters and hot summers. Enough rain falls to make the grass grow, but there is not enough rain for large trees. **Decayed** grass roots make dark, rich soil.

North American plain or prairie

Grasslands go by many names in other places.

Country	Name
South Africa	veldts
Hungary	puszta
Argentina	pampas
Russia	steppes
United States	plains or prairies

Grasses Come and Go

Winter brings cold weather and wind. The grasses dry. Snow covers the grass.

Bison have thick fur that protects them against the cold.

prairie dogs

Many grassland animals move to warmer places or hibernate during the winter. But bison and prairie dogs stay on the prairie all winter.

In spring, melting snow soaks the land. Flowers open. The grasses grow. Rain comes late in spring.

Prairie flowers like coneflowers, goldenrods, asters, clovers, blazing stars, and wild indigos grow among the grasses.

Grasses grow swiftly and many young animals are born.

Pronghorns are very fast runners. Baby pronghorns can outrun a human just a few days after they are born.

The hot, windy summer is a time of growth on the **prairie**.

Little bluestem   Indian grass

Little and big bluestem and Indian grass are prairie grasses.

Many kinds of grasses make up grasslands.
They grow thick root mats below the soil.

The thick tangle of roots under the ground quickly soaks up water. The roots also allow the plant to grow again after winter or any fires that pass through.

In fall, the grasses dry. Plants turn golden.

While grasslands are mostly flat, some have hills.

Lightning strikes often cause grassland fires during the dry times of the year.

Seasonal fires are important to keep balance in plants and animals living in the grasslands.

Living on the Grasslands

In North America, animals that **graze** live on the grasslands. Prairie dogs dig tunnels and **burrow** under the ground.

Tule elk live in the grasslands of California.

Coyotes, foxes, and bobcats hunt in the grasslands. They look for mice and other small creatures that hide in the grass.

With its terrific sense of smell and keen hearing, the coyote finds it easy to locate prey in the grassland.

Grasshoppers, crickets, beetles, snakes, lizards, and worms become food for many birds.

Birds will often come to the site of a grassland fire searching for easy prey like the grasshopper.

The Northern harrier has feathers around its face that focus sound into its ears.

Future of Grasslands

Grasslands make fine farm land. Crops of corn and wheat grow well in the rich soil. Ranchers graze cattle and sheep on the thick grass.

American prairies are often called the breadbasket of the world because of the large amounts of grain they produce.

But clearing away too many grasslands makes loose soil. It blows away in the wind. Plants cannot grow and animals lose their homes.

Conservation groups are teaching people about the value of grasslands. They are trying to help find a balance between human needs and nature's needs.

Bison once filled the prairies. Too much hunting almost killed them all. Today, the number of bison is growing and people are learning how to manage bison.

Grasslands are an important part of our world. Help keep them healthy.

You Can Help
Protect Grasslands:
✓ Write letters to leaders telling why we need to conserve our grasslands.
✓ Join a prairie restoration group.
✓ Donate to help save grasslands.
✓ Conserve energy to reduce global warming.

Grasslands are the most endangered biome in the world. We need to do all we can to protect them.

Study Like a Scientist
It's All in the Roots

1. Pull up a small square of grass.

2. Put it on white paper.

3. Spread out the roots.

4. Draw them.

5. What do the grass roots look like?

The roots branch out like the grass roots in grasslands.

Glossary

burrow (BUR-oh): an underground tunnel or hole where animals live

decayed (di-KAYD): broken down or rotten

grasshoppers (GRAS-hah-purz): jumping insects with long back legs that eat grass

grasslands (GRAS-landz): wide open land filled with grasses and having few or no trees

graze (GRAZE): to eat grass growing in a field or prairie

prairie (PRAIR-ee): another name for grasslands

Index

Websites

www.enchantedlearning.com/biomes/grassland/grassland.shtml

kids.nceas.ucsb.edu/biomes/grassland.html

amhistory.si.edu/ourstory/activities/sodhouse/more.html

About the Author

Shirley Duke has written many books about science. She lives in Texas and New Mexico and loves the different seasons in each place. She visited a tall grass prairie farm where the grass came up to her waist. She thinks she would not like living in a sod house, but enjoys learning about the many kinds of grasses.

Meet The Author!
www.meetREMauthors.com